Shawn Mendes Coloring Book

Canadian Pop Rock Sensation and PostBieber Era of Talented Youtubers Inspired Adult Coloring Book

Monica Clinton

SHAWN
Mendes

SHAWN
MENDES

SHAWN
MENDES

SHAWN MENDES
HANDWRITTEN

Shawn Mende

HD

Made in the USA
San Bernardino, CA
03 October 2017